W9-CLN-108

TUSCARAWAS COUNTY PUBLIC LIBRARY

3 1342 00195 4402

DATE DUE

9 9

LINDBERGH, CHARLES

cop. 1

jB   Collins, David R.
 LIN   Charles Lindbergh

TUSCARAWAS CO. PUBLIC LIBRARY
121 Fair Ave., N.W.
New Phila., OH 44663

County

A Discovery Biography

Charles Lindbergh

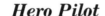

Hero Pilot

by David R. Collins
illustrated by Victor Mays

TUSCARAWAS CO. PUBLIC LIBRARY
121 Fair Ave., N.W.
New Phila., OH 44663
County

CHELSEA JUNIORS
A division of Chelsea House Publishers
New York • Philadelphia

This book is dedicated to Evelyn Witter, who has
provided "flight instructions" to countless beginning
writers

The Discovery Books have been prepared under the
educational supervision of Mary C. Austin, Ed.D.,
Reading Specialist and Professor of Education, Case
Western Reserve University.

Cover illustration: Paul Chadwick

First Chelsea House edition 1991

Copyright © MCMXCI by Chelsea House Publishers, a division
of Main Line Book Co. All rights reserved. Printed and bound in
the United States of America.
© MCMLXXVIII by David R. Collins

3 5 7 9 8 6 4

ISBN 0-7910-1417-7

Contents

Chapter *1*

A Special Place

Charles Augustus Lindbergh climbed up happily, using the wooden "steps" he had nailed to the tree trunk. The eight-year-old boy finally reached his lookout high up in the tree.

He could hear the rushing sound of the Mississippi River which came from the distance. The boy watched the afternoon wind as it played through the leaves on the trees. It was summertime in Minnesota. The year was 1910.

"Are you going to stay up there all day?"

Charles looked down at his friend, Bill Thompson.

"Everybody's going to go swimming," Bill called. "Want to come?"

Charles shook his head. "Not right now. Maybe in a little while."

Although Charles liked to swim with his friends, he wanted to be alone in his lookout a little longer.

His father would have understood. Charles Lindbergh, Sr., had taught his son to love the quiet of the woods. "Get to know nature," his father had told him. "Learn about the world around you. That way your life will always be interesting and exciting."

Mr. Lindbergh had taught Charles to know the forest plants and animals. He had also taught him to fish and swim. Once when Charles was first learning to swim, he stepped into a deep hole.

Frightened, he splashed his arms back and forth. Suddenly his feet touched ground again. Why, he'd been swimming, Charles realized with pride. His father stood smiling on shore.

"Good work!" Mr. Lindbergh called. "You got yourself into trouble, and you got yourself out. Remember, always be able to take care of yourself."

Now from his tree, Charles took a last look at a friendly squirrel. Then the boy climbed down and raced home.

His mother sat reading a book on the front porch.

"I'm going swimming," Charles told her as he leaped up the porch steps.

Evangeline Lindbergh nodded. "Yes, enjoy these few weeks all you can," she said. "We'll soon be going back to Washington."

Charles slowed his steps as he walked

to his room. He did not want to think about leaving their farm, Lindholm. Mr. Lindbergh was a member of the United States House of Representatives. Most of the year the Lindbergh family lived in Washington, D.C.

Charles did not like the noisy, crowded city. Here at Lindholm he could hike and camp out. There were always new trails to enjoy, new things to discover.

Charles went to his dresser to get a dry swimming suit. He stopped to look at a pile of pebbles on the top of the dresser. The sunlight made the brightly colored stones sparkle.

Suddenly he heard a noise outside. As he listened it became louder. It sounded like an engine. The boy rushed to the window and climbed out onto the roof.

Charles could see an airplane in the distance. It would fly over his house!

Airplanes were very new at that time, and there were few of them. Charles had seen some at a flying show in Virginia. But here was an airplane in Minnesota!

At first the small plane circled the nearby town of Little Falls. Then it flew low up the river. Soon it was so close Charles could clearly see the pilot.

Charles waved excitedly. As the plane flew over the trees, he watched every move it made.

Finally, when the airplane was out of sight, Charles climbed back into his room and raced downstairs. His mother was standing at the doorway.

"Did you see the airplane?" the boy asked. "Where did it come from?"

"There is a story in the newspaper," said Mrs. Lindbergh. "Some man has come here to take people up in his plane."

"Do you think I could go up with him?" Charles asked.

"No, Charles. Flying is not for eight-year-old boys."

"But—"

"No, Charles," Mrs. Lindbergh said firmly. She turned and walked away.

Slowly the boy went into the front yard. His plans for going swimming were forgotten. He looked up at the sky and hoped the airplane would return.

"Someday," Charles whispered to himself. "Someday I'm going to fly."

Chapter 2

Fun with Machines

One morning Charles was busy cleaning his bicycle chain. He was fourteen now, and he enjoyed working with mechanical things.

The farmhouse was empty. Charles's mother and two older halfsisters were out. Mr. and Mrs. Lindbergh were now separated, and Charles's father spent most of his time in Washington.

Suddenly Charles's dog, Dingo, began to bark.

"You know who is coming, don't you boy?" Charles laughed.

An automobile appeared down the road. The car was his father's. Mr. Lindbergh had called the night before to tell Charles he was coming. Quickly Charles grabbed a catalog from the porch and raced to the roadside.

"I'm looking for a good driver to show me around this farm," Mr. Lindbergh said. His eyes twinkled.

"I will!" Charles answered. He handed the catalog to his father. "While I drive, will you please look at the page I have marked?"

Charles climbed into his father's car and started the engine. In those days there was no minimum age for driving, and Charles had learned when he was eleven. Even then his long legs reached the pedals easily.

After driving the car past the barn, Charles stopped at the side of the road.

"Would you order that tractor for the farm?" Charles pointed at a picture in the catalog. "When the company sends the parts, I know I can put it together."

Mr. Lindbergh looked closely at the picture. He knew Charles liked to work with machines. He had watched his son use only minutes to take rifles apart and put them together. Once the boy had even fixed a broken water pump that no one else could fix. But could he build a tractor?

"I'll keep up with my chores," Charles promised. "Please let me try."

Mr. Lindbergh smiled and shook hands with his son. "It's a deal, Charles."

As soon as the parts arrived, Charles went right to work. He read and reread the instructions. Hour after hour he worked in the barn. Finally, after three

16

days, Charles drove the new machine out of the barn.

Mr. Lindbergh was very proud of his son. Charles was delighted when his father bought him a motorcycle. The boy rode it to Little Falls High School—and everywhere he went.

While Charles was attending high school, America went to war. Many farmers left to fight in Europe. Yet farm goods were badly needed. Charles worked hard raising crops and livestock. He had little time for schoolwork, but in June 1918, when he was sixteen, Charles graduated from high school.

Charles had given little thought to his future. Although he enjoyed working out-doors at Lindholm, he knew he did not want to farm all his life. He decided to give college a try.

Charles soon knew he had made the

wrong decision. None of his courses interested him. Besides, he did not like to study. Often he just closed his books and went riding on his motorcycle.

One afternoon Charles and some friends stopped their motorcycles at the top of a big hill.

"I think I can go down this hill without using my brakes," Charles said.

"No, you can't!" one of his friends cried. "You'll have to slow down at the bottom to get around that turn. If you don't, you'll end up in the hospital."

Charles shook his head. "I'm going to prove you're wrong," he said. Slowly he rolled forward on his bike. Down the hill he raced, going faster and faster.

At the bottom, Charles leaned to one side and turned his bike sharply. The motorcycle spun out from under him. Charles was thrown against a fence.

Dazed, he sat up and rubbed his head. His friends ran to help him. "You know," Charles said thoughtfully. "That wouldn't have happened if I'd gunned the motor just as I made my turn."

Charles checked his motorcycle carefully. It wasn't hurt, so he rode it to the top of the hill. He wanted to try again.

This time when he reached the bottom, he raced the motor. He made it around the turn.

"I did it!" Charles shouted. "I did it!"

Charles knew he was wasting his time in college. Finally he decided to leave and take flying lessons. Surely that would be more exciting!

"Flying is too dangerous for you," Mr. Lindbergh said. "You're my only son, and I don't want to lose you. Airplanes are just wood and canvas tied together with wire. Why not give farming another try?"

But Charles did not change his mind. His mother understood.

"You must lead your own life," she told her son.

There were no regular flying schools then, but Charles had heard that an airplane company in Lincoln, Nebraska, was looking for student pilots. Eagerly, Charles filled his motorcycle with gas and headed for Nebraska.

Chapter *3*

Into the Air

Charles and another student walked around the small plane on the field. It belonged to the airplane company. Lovingly, Charles touched the canvas cloth that covered the plane's light wooden body.

"All set, Slim?"

Charles turned to greet his teacher. The workers in the plane factory liked the tall, slender boy from Minnesota. They had nicknamed him Slim.

Now Slim and the other student took their places in the front cockpit. It was open, as was the rear cockpit, in which the flying instructor sat. The instructor waved to a mechanic to spin the propeller and start the engine.

Charles's heart pounded faster as the plane rolled forward. The instructor turned the plane into the wind. The engine roared as the plane bounced down the bumpy field. Takeoff! For the first time in his life, Charles was flying. He felt as free as a bird.

As the plane climbed higher, Charles looked around. He was in a wonderful world of clouds and open space. The air rushing against his cheeks made him feel fresh and alive. A heavy wind shook the little plane, and it dropped suddenly before the pilot gained control. Charles looked back at the pilot. One wrong move and the flight could end in death. But that only added to Charles's excitement.

When the first lesson was over, Charles could hardly wait for the next one. He was a good student, always listening to his instructor and carrying out his orders. Soon the instructor let Charles do the flying when they went up.

By the end of six weeks, Charles was ready to solo, to fly a plane by himself. But he did not get the chance then. Since there were no other student pilots, the airplane company closed the school. The training plane was put up for sale. A man named Erold Bahl bought it for "barnstorming," or stunt flying.

In the 1920s pilots often flew from place to place and put on air shows. Planes were still so new, many people had never seen one.

Charles did not want to give up flying. So he asked Bahl to let him go on the barnstorming trip. Bahl agreed.

Each day Charles made sure Bahl's plane was clean. He took money from people who wanted a ride. He spun the propeller when Bahl was ready to go up. In return, Bahl taught him a lot about flying. Charles often flew the plane as the two men moved about the country. Bahl liked his helper, and he trusted him.

One night Charles and Bahl sat by a campfire after dinner.

"Before we land in the next town, I'll stand up between the wings," Charles suggested. "More people will watch us come in. I'll bet the crowd will double."

Early the next morning the two men took off. Soon they were flying over a big county fairground.

Carefully Charles climbed out of the front cockpit. Holding onto the thin wires between the plane's wings, he moved slowly out onto the lower wing.

People watched from the ground below. A ride on the Ferris wheel did not compare with the sky ride they could watch for free.

"Look at that fellow on the wing!" someone cried. "He doesn't have a parachute!"

For several minutes Bahl circled the fairgrounds. Charles smiled and waved to the crowd below. When the plane landed, hundreds of people gathered around it.

"Your idea sure worked, Slim," Bahl yelled.

After a month of barnstorming, Charles and Bahl returned to Lincoln. Charles went to work at the airplane factory. He learned how all the parts of the plane were made. He learned how to put them together. Soon he began saving money for his own plane.

One afternoon a parachute salesman,

Charles Hardin, came to the airfield. The man went up in a plane to make a jump. Charles watched as the parachute ballooned open. Hardin drifted slowly to the ground. It looked like fun.

"Will you teach me to jump?" Charles asked Hardin. "I've heard you can use as many parachutes as you want. I'd like to try it with two parachutes. I think it would be even more exciting than with one."

Hardin said that jumping with two parachutes would be difficult for someone learning to jump. Still, he agreed to show Charles how to do it.

"Two parachutes will be packed together," said Hardin. "First one will open. Then you will cut away from it, and fall free until the second takes over. The rest is up to you."

Charles listened closely to all of the

directions. The next day he was ready to go up.

The pilot took the plane up to 2,000 feet. When it was time, Charles climbed out of the front cockpit. Holding on to the wires, he moved carefully to the end of the wing.

As the pilot slowed the plane, Charles swung under the wing. He jumped free, turning in open space. The first parachute opened above him. He breathed deeply, enjoying every minute of the trip downward. It was time to open the second chute. Charles cut the first chute away, and then pulled the cord for the second. Nothing happened. He dropped faster and faster.

Then there was a sudden jerk. The full white parachute floated above him. Calmly Charles took out a small camera and began taking pictures.

Seconds later he was on the ground. Hardin was the first to reach him.

"I thought that second parachute would never open. I'm sorry," Hardin said. "I couldn't find the twine to tie the two chutes together. So I used heavy string. I thought it would be okay, but it must have broken. I'm really sorry."

But Charles was not listening. He hardly heard the people around him. He was lost in his own thoughts as he looked up at the sky. It was more than just air and clouds.

The sky was his friend.

Chapter 4

Thrills and Spills

That first parachute jump made Charles sure that he wanted to spend more time in the sky. Nothing else could possibly be as exciting.

Soon a pilot named Cupid Lynch gave Charles the chance he wanted. Cupid and Charles worked in the airplane factory together. He asked Charles to go barnstorming with him.

"You do the tricks, and I'll do the flying," Cupid told Charles. "We'll call you Daredevil Lindbergh."

Together the men traveled across the Midwest. Charles made friends with other stunt flyers, who taught him new tricks. His favorite was one where he appeared to hang from a wing by his teeth. Actually, he was held by a thin wire that ran from the wing to the harness under his jacket.

"You sure make those crowds scream," Cupid laughed.

A wide grin crossed Charles's face. "The funny thing is that I feel safer in the air than I do on the ground."

Charles liked working with Cupid. But he was 21 now, and he wanted his own plane. In the spring of 1923 he learned that old army planes were being sold in Georgia. Charles went to the sale. For $500 he bought his first plane.

Charles had been flying for over a year now. But he still had never flown solo.

On an April morning Charles climbed into the cockpit of his plane. He tried to remember everything from his flying lessons in Nebraska. He thought about what Erold Bahl had taught him, too. Carefully Charles started his plane as a mechanic spun the propeller.

Charles's heart pounded faster as he taxied his plane across the field. He headed the plane into the wind to take off.

For a moment the plane was in the air. Then it hit the ground and finally came to a stop. Charles sat there, wondering what he had done wrong.

A pilot came running over to see if he could help. "Why don't we go up together," he suggested. "You'll get used to this plane soon."

All morning the man and Charles practiced takeoffs and landings.

Later that afternoon, Charles climbed into his plane alone and took off easily. Upward, skyward, the plane climbed to 4,000 feet, then 5,000. Charles felt like a bird, turning, gliding, dipping in the air. He played tag with the clouds and hide-and-seek with the sun. When he finally landed on the field, Charles knew he would never forget his first solo flight.

Now that he had his own plane, Charles flew back and forth across the country. To earn money he barnstormed and took passengers on short trips.

Wherever Charles went, he talked with other pilots. One of them had just gradu-ated from an Army Air Service school.

"You should go there," the young man told Charles. "The instructors are great, and you get to fly the best planes."

It sounded like a good idea to Charles. As new planes were built, there was more

to learn about flying. In March 1924 he became an air service cadet at Brooks Field in San Antonio, Texas.

Charles was allowed to solo on the first day of flight training. He passed the loop and spin tests easily. There was also classroom work. Charles learned about motors and radios and attended classes in aviation science. For the first time in his life, he worked at his classroom studies.

One hundred and four men started the training program with Charles. Six months later only 33 were left. The rest had not passed the tests.

The 33 students moved to Kelly Field, ten miles away, to finish their training. Classroom work was harder. New, high-powered planes were used for flying. Often the students flew in formation.

One afternoon Charles was flying with eight other students. They were pretending to chase an enemy plane. Suddenly he heard a terrible noise. Charles's plane seemed to turn and stop in the air.

Charles looked around. There, only a few feet away, was another plane. Charles saw that the wings of the two planes were locked together.

There was no choice but to parachute out. Quickly both pilots leaped from their planes.

As Charles drifted down, his parachute open, he watched the other pilot drifting above him. Their two planes sped toward the ground and burst into flames.

Charles and the other pilot landed in a field. They were the first two men ever to escape alive from airplanes which had collided in the sky.

A week later Charles graduated from the Army Air Service Training School. He was the top man in his class.

Chapter *5*

Carrying the Mail

After graduation, Charles became an officer in the air force reserve. He could be called back to active duty in time of war.

Shortly after that, Charles met Bill and Frank Robertson, who owned a small airplane factory in St. Louis.

"The government is trying to set up an airmail service across the country," Bill told Charles. "Our company hopes to get the route between St. Louis and Chicago. If we do, we want you to be our chief pilot."

The Robertsons were given the mail route. Charles agreed to take the job. First, he picked out nine landing fields between St. Louis and Chicago where the planes could stop if necessary. Each field had a telephone and gas. Then Charles hired two more pilots to help carry the mail.

In April of 1926 Charles loaded the front cockpit of his plane with mail bags. Then he climbed in the rear cockpit and took off. Airmail service between St. Louis and Chicago had begun. Soon there were five round trips each week.

Charles was proud of the service. A letter mailed in St. Louis one day could reach New York or Los Angeles in 24 hours. When a Robertson plane landed in Chicago, another mail plane was ready to take off for the east or west coast.

But the Robertsons had problems with the service. Many St. Louis businessmen did not want to pay extra for airmail. Often the mail bags were almost empty. The service was not paying for itself.

One night Charles found himself in a

thick fog near Chicago. He could see no lights to guide him down. He dropped a lighted flare, but it did not help.

Then the airplane engine began to miss. Gas was running low. Still Charles could not find a place to land. Twenty minutes passed. Charles headed the plane away from the city. If he were going to crash, he did not want anyone else to be hurt or killed.

Suddenly the airplane engine died. Charles climbed from his cockpit and jumped. His parachute opened.

Without warning, the plane started up again and circled wildly. It missed hitting Charles by only a hundred yards. Finally it disappeared and crashed below.

Charles found a farmer who helped him find the plane. Charles picked up the mail bags and hurried to a train station. He sent the mail on to Chicago.

In his free time Charles read about new airplanes. Single-wing planes were replacing the old double-wing planes. Engines were better planned to give greater speed and power. Closed cockpits offered pilots safety from bad weather.

One new airplane became Charles's favorite. It was called the "Bellanca," and it carried a fine engine made by the Wright Company. Charles was sure the Bellanca could do almost anything.

"I could fly for miles with a plane like that," Charles thought excitedly one night as he flew the mail route. He looked out at the beckoning stars. "I could even fly from New York City to Paris, France!"

Chapter 6

The Prize

Charles moved restlessly as he sat waiting to talk with Earl Thompson.

Mr. Thompson was a rich insurance man in St. Louis, who loved flying. Now Charles hoped Mr. Thompson would help him make a special flight.

The first pilot to fly nonstop across the Atlantic Ocean between New York and Paris would win $25,000. A Frenchman named Raymond Orteig had put up the prize money. He hoped the flight would strengthen friendship between the French people and the Americans. Orteig also wanted to encourage flying.

Orteig had first made his offer in 1919. For five years no one tried to win the money. The distance between New York and France was over 3,300 miles. Planes had not been built to fly that far.

In 1924 Orteig made his offer again. Airplane engines were more powerful, and pilots were better trained. But something else was needed for a pilot to try for the Orteig prize—courage. Charles did not fear the long flight. Yet he knew he had to have a good plane. And a good plane would cost a lot of money.

By the fall of 1926 Charles had saved $2,000. But he needed at least $15,000. He decided to ask businessmen in St. Louis for help.

Finally Earl Thompson came into the room. The two men shook hands. Then they started to talk about what Charles wanted to do.

"I think a Wright-Bellanca airplane can make that flight," Charles said. "I'd like to try it. It would show people what airplanes can do."

Mr. Thompson nodded. "That plane has only one engine, hasn't it?"

"Yes, that means it's not as heavy as a two or three-engine plane. It can carry more gas."

For hours the men talked. After he left, Charles went to visit other people who might be able to help him.

But not everyone he talked to was as friendly as Mr. Thompson.

"A one-engine plane could *never* make such a trip!" said one newspaper editor. "It's a wild idea!"

But slowly Charles began to win people over. One man gave him $200. Another gave $1,000.

But time was running out. Other flyers

47

were making plans for the flight. One of them, Rene Fonck, had tried once and failed. Yet the French war ace was getting ready to try again.

Richard E. Byrd had become famous as the first man to reach the North Pole by plane. Now he planned to win the Orteig prize. Each week the newspapers carried more stories about pilots testing their planes for the flight to Paris.

At last Charles was ready to ask the Wright Company to build a special Bellanca for him.

"We're sorry," an official told Charles. "We only built that plane to show people what fine engines we make. We have many orders for our engines. We are not interested in building a plane for you."

"Then I'll find another company that will build the airplane I want," Charles answered.

It was not easy. At 25, Charles was unknown to most airplane builders. When he told them he was sure he could fly the Atlantic alone in a one-engine plane, they shook their heads.

Finally, Ryan Airlines in San Diego, California, agreed. Quickly Charles flew to San Diego. He wanted to be sure the plane would be built just the way he wanted. He helped with the design. The plane would have a strong, 200-horsepower engine. It would have two huge gas tanks in front of the enclosed cockpit. There would be three more in the wings. Charles knew every detail he wanted in his flying machine. The workmen listened to him carefully.

By April 1927 the plane was finished. The small silver craft was 9 feet, 10 inches high and 27 feet, 8 inches long. Charles watched proudly as the name was painted

on the body. The *Spirit of St. Louis* honored the people who had put up the money.

On May 10, Charles took off from San Diego. Fourteen hours later he landed the *Spirit of St. Louis* in St. Louis. His trip there broke two records. It was farther than any one pilot had flown before non-stop—and faster too. After a day's rest, he left for New York.

There, Charles studied maps and charts and weather conditions. He checked all the parts of his plane and made some test flights.

One morning Charles received a telegram. His mother was coming to see him off. He knew she was worried about his safety.

In less than nine months, six brave men had died trying to make the flight over the Atlantic Ocean. Two planes had

TUSCARAWAS COUNTY PUBLIC LIBRARY
County

crashed soon after takeoff, and four flyers had been killed. Two more men had gone down somewhere at sea. "Will Charles Lindbergh Be Unlucky Number Seven?" one newspaper headline asked.

Charles welcomed his mother warmly. Proudly he took her to see his plane, and he explained his plans. He wished his father had lived to share the excitement, but Mr. Lindbergh had died three years before. When Charles said good-bye to his mother, she was less worried about the planned flight.

Each day Charles watched the weather reports closely. His plane was ready. But the sky over the Atlantic must be clear for the trip.

Charles wanted to be sure he was *not* "Unlucky Number Seven."

Chapter 7

Long Flight

It was May 20, 1927. Charles stepped out of a car on the runway at Roosevelt Field on Long Island. The early morning air was cool and misty. The sky was filled with thick clouds.

A worker on the field stepped forward. "We hear the weather is better where you're headed, sir."

Charles smiled and nodded. "That's what I've heard. I hope it's true."

The *Spirit of St. Louis* was filled with gas. The tanks were so full that the tires bulged from the extra weight.

Charles carefully checked over his airplane. The propeller, the brakes, the wings—everything seemed to be in top condition.

The field was soft from the rain that had been falling. Was it hard enough for takeoff? The way to find out was to try.

Charles returned to the car that had brought him to the field. He slipped his flying suit over his clothes. Then he put on his helmet and goggles.

A crowd of people stood nearby. They watched silently.

Charles walked to the airplane and climbed into the cockpit. He signaled to the ground crew to spin the propeller. The motor coughed a bit and then roared into life.

"The engine's turning a bit slow," a mechanic said. "It's the wetness in the air."

An overloaded airplane—a soft runway—a slow engine. The thoughts raced through Charles's mind. He pulled his safety belt tight and lowered his goggles. He had no parachute, for one weighed twenty pounds. All extras on the plane had been removed so he could carry more gas.

The *Spirit of St. Louis* moved forward like a heavy truck. The wheels cut into the mud. Still, the airplane gained speed. Finally Charles pulled the throttle back. The wheels left the ground.

Slowly the *Spirit of St. Louis* climbed higher. Below him Charles could see the faces of the watching people.

Charles looked at the instrument board. The plane was headed north and flying at over 100 miles an hour. The time was 7:54 A.M., Eastern Daylight Time.

Charles settled back in his cockpit seat. Soon he saw farms and woodlands below.

The minutes ticked away. The *Spirit of St. Louis* passed over New England and flew on to Canada—Nova Scotia and then Newfoundland. Just before dark, Charles said a silent, last farewell to land. Only the Atlantic Ocean lay ahead.

He looked about. Above him, clouds hid the moon from sight. Below, great icebergs floated in the northern waters.

Finally the moon appeared again. Stars twinkled in the dark sky as the hours rolled by.

Suddenly a thick storm cloud closed around the plane. Charles pulled his safety belt tighter. The air within the storm cloud shook the plane.

Charles pulled off his glove and put his hand through the window. It was sleeting!

Turning on his flashlight, he saw that ice covered the wings.

There was no time to lose. The weight

of the ice could send the plane crashing into the water. Charles turned the *Spirit of St. Louis* around. He must get out of the ice storm quickly.

Back in the clear air, the ice on the wings soon melted. But now the plane was headed for America. Carefully Charles steered his plane around the storm cloud.

Other clouds appeared. They helped keep Charles alert and awake. Sometimes he flew low to miss them. Other times he flew above them. It was like a game. But he, the lone player, could make no mistake.

Charles checked the time. He had been in the air 20 hours. He stretched his stiff, tired body. He turned his head from side to side, fighting away sleep.

Closely Charles studied his instruments. He wondered if he were now halfway to France. There was no way to be sure.

Radios then could only send messages short distances. He had decided against bringing one.

Charles thought of his childhood. He remembered hiking and camping in Minnesota. He remembered his parents, the first plane he had seen in Little Falls, his motorcycle. He wrote down all his thoughts in a notebook. It helped to make the hours pass more quickly.

On and on the *Spirit of St. Louis* flew. Finally, after 27 hours in the air, Charles spotted some black dots on the water.

His heart pounded. His eyes widened.

"They're fishing boats!" he exclaimed.

The excited pilot dipped his plane and circled 50 feet above the boats. Charles saw a man looking up.

"Which way is Ireland?" Charles called down.

The fisherman did not answer. Again

Charles shouted the question. Still there was no answer. Maybe the man could not hear.

Charles lifted his plane skyward and continued his trip.

An hour later, Ireland's rocky coast was a happy sight. The excitement made Charles feel less sleepy.

On to England Charles flew. Then he flew across the English Channel. He checked his maps to make sure he was on course.

Oh, how good it would feel to lie down. Charles slapped his cheeks to stay alert. He had not slept in over 30 hours. Surely it could not be much further to Paris.

From a nearby bag Charles took a sandwich. The ham and bread had little taste. He took a drink of water from his thermos.

Charles knew when he was over France. He had spent hours looking at pictures and maps. Just a little farther—a few more miles—yes, there it was. The lights of Le Bourget Airport in Paris shone in the darkness.

Charles circled the airport. Slowly he dropped lower. At 10:24 P.M., Paris time, on May 21, 1927, the *Spirit of St. Louis* landed. The 3,600-mile flight had taken 33½ hours.

Chapter *8*

In the Headlines

As the *Spirit of St. Louis* rolled to a stop, Charles could not believe what he saw. Thousands of people were running toward him. "Lindbergh!" they shouted, dashing forward. "Lindbergh!"

His plane had been seen, and the news that he was over Paris had been broadcast everywhere.

Charles heard wood cracking. Some of the people wanted a piece of the *Spirit of St. Louis* as a souvenir.

"Does anyone here speak English?" Charles yelled.

The men and women shouted louder, but no one answered Charles's question.

He felt his airplane shake. Surely someone would help him save it.

Charles climbed out of the cockpit. Quickly the crowd lifted him high into the air. They cheered and carried him around the plane.

Finally, two French pilots came to help

Charles out of the crowd. Police surrounded his plane. Charles was taken to a building where he met the American ambassador.

"You'll stay with me in Paris," the ambassador said.

The plane was put in a hangar under heavy guard. Charles was driven to the American Embassy, where he went to bed.

When Charles awoke, people filled the streets in front of the embassy. Newspapermen begged to speak with America's new hero.

"You might as well get used to all this attention," the American ambassador told Charles. "You are going to get a lot more of it."

How true those words were.

When Charles left France, he went to Belgium and then on to England. In each city where he stopped, he was given medals and gifts. He ate with kings and queens. Every night there were parties in his honor.

Americans were eager to welcome home the country's flying ace. People everywhere sang the song "Lucky Lindy," written in Charles's honor. The "Lone Eagle" became his nickname.

President Coolidge of the United States sent a ship to bring Charles and the *Spirit of St. Louis* home. On June 11, 1927, the ship sailed up the Potomac River to Washington, D.C. More than a hundred planes, flying in perfect formation, filled the sky. Cannons boomed. Flags flew from every pole.

As the ship docked, Charles saw his mother waiting to see him. A program in Charles's honor was held in front of the Washington Monument.

"We are proud and happy to welcome

you back," said President Calvin Coolidge. From a small box, he took a new medal called the Distinguished Flying Cross. The president pinned it on Charles's coat.

From Washington, D.C., Charles went to New York City. There four million people cheered as he rode in a parade with the mayor. Paper floated from high windows.

"This is worse than the snowstorms I've flown in," Charles joked. He waved to the crowds, his boyish grin delighting the people.

Charles felt he owed a special treat to the people of St. Louis. He flew a plane over the city.

Wherever Charles went, crowds gathered. People begged for his autograph. They sent him presents and letters. Proud parents named their babies after him. City officials named streets and avenues for him.

"Charles Lindbergh belongs to all of us," wrote one newspaperman. "He is a member of each American family. He is the son and brother every American would like to have."

At first Charles enjoyed the attention he received. He was especially happy to see the new interest people had in flying.

But slowly Charles grew tired of being in the newspapers. He could not go to a restaurant without reporters coming to his table. Photographers were always taking his picture. A movie company offered him a million dollars to act in a movie. He liked talking about airplanes, but did not enjoy talking about himself.

Job offers came in from every major American airline. Each one wanted Charles to promote flying by piloting the *Spirit of St. Louis* across the country. The airlines wanted him to plan new flight routes too. Charles was happy to take a job with Pan American Airlines.

Back and forth Charles flew across the country. He made new friends everywhere. One of them was a rich banker named Dwight Morrow, who invited Charles to visit his home.

Mr. Morrow had a 21-year-old daughter, Anne, whom Charles especially enjoyed. She was shy and quiet like Charles, but she had a quick mind and warm smile. Soon Charles knew he was in love. In May of 1929, Charles Lindbergh and Anne Morrow were married. They settled in New Jersey.

Anne told Charles she wanted to learn to fly. He was delighted and became her teacher. She also spent much of her time writing. She hoped to become an author.

In June 1930 Charles and Anne had a son, Charles A. Lindbergh III.

A year later Charles was busy planning an air route across Canada to China. Charles and Anne decided to fly to China together. Anne would take notes on the trip and write a book about it later.

After Charles and Anne returned home, tragedy struck.

On the night of March 1, 1932, young Charles Lindbergh III was kidnapped. Later the kidnapper sent a note, asking for a large sum of money.

Charles and Anne paid the money, for they were willing to do anything to get their baby back.

But later the body of their 20-month-old baby was found—dead.

Cards and letters came from people all over the world. Everyone wanted the Lindberghs to know how bad they felt about the baby. But words could not help the sadness of the lonely parents.

Chapter 9

War and Peace

Late in 1932, another Lindbergh baby was born. Jon Morrow brought new happiness to his parents. But the kidnapping of their first son had changed Charles and Anne. They kept more to themselves.

Charles had some new work now. Dr. Alexis Carrel had asked Charles to help him develop a special pump to be used during hospital operations.

During this time, the search for the kidnapper of the Lindbergh baby went on. When the kidnapper was found, there was a long trial. Reporters followed Charles everywhere. He hated the newspaper stories, and he worried about little Jon. Charles was afraid of another kidnapping.

To keep his family safe, Charles moved them to England. Later they rented a house on an island off France. Soon another son, Land, was born. Later the Lindberghs had two daughters and another son.

While Charles was abroad, he was invited to visit other countries and see their airplanes. He became very worried by what he saw in Germany. The German leaders were building thousands of fighter planes and bombers.

Charles went to see the leaders of the British and French governments. He warned them about Germany's air power. But the British and French leaders would not listen.

In 1939, Charles moved his family back to the United States. That summer, World War II started in Europe.

"We must not get into the war," Charles warned the people of America. "Germany will soon control Europe. We must not waste lives and money fighting a useless battle."

Many Americans believed Charles was wrong. They wanted to help the people of Europe.

In 1941 the United States entered the war. At once Charles offered his services to the government.

President Franklin Roosevelt would not accept Charles's offer.

But Charles was determined to serve his country. He went to work for private companies that were building war planes. He helped design bomber planes and planned speed tests for fighter planes.

Later on, during the war, he was asked to study one of the planes in action. He went to the South Pacific as a civilian, and he flew in 50 combat missions.

For four years, the war dragged on. Finally, in August 1945, it ended.

Happily Charles returned to his family, who now lived in a house on the Connecticut shore. He could swim and sail there with his children. In the winter, they often went on skiing trips.

Charles continued to work for major airlines. He helped chart air routes and design planes.

The United States started new programs in rocket and space travel. Charles was asked to help. Sometimes he represented the United States at meetings with flight officials in other countries. He was always willing to work hard to make flying more successful.

Chapter *10*

Final Journey

Charles Lindbergh stood in the middle of a big stage. He was talking to a group of high school students.

"It is up to you to use nature wisely," he said, "and to protect it."

The students listened closely. The year was 1972. It was hard to believe the man talking was 70 years old. Somehow his age was hidden behind his sparkling eyes and boyish grin.

"Once the American eagle disappears from our world, we can never get him back. The same is true of the polar bear—or a fresh water lake—or a patch of rich soil."

Most of Charles's time now was spent working for conservation. His articles about saving animals, land, and water were read by millions of people. He drew big crowds wherever he spoke about protecting nature.

The Lindbergh children were grown now, and all of them were married. But they frequently gathered at the family home in Connecticut.

Charles and Anne had a new vacation home on the island of Maui in Hawaii. It was quiet and peaceful, a perfect spot for writing and enjoying nature.

In 1974 Charles went to see his doctor in New York. The doctor told Charles he had cancer and would not have long to live.

"I will put you in a hospital," said the doctor.

Charles shook his head. "No," he said firmly. "I want to be at home with my family."

On August 26, 1974, Charles Lindbergh died in Hawaii. Around the world newspapers and newscasts carried the sad news. Stories told of the young, brave pilot who had flown alone across the Atlantic from America to France. Many reminded people that his famous plane, the *Spirit of St. Louis,* can still be seen in the Smithsonian Institution, a Washington museum that Charles visited as a boy.

President Ford remembered the flying ace. "Charles Lindbergh represented all that was best in our country—honesty, courage, and the will to greatness."

A simple service was held in a small Hawaiian church. As the people left, many of them gazed upward. Across the sky flew a lone plane. It reminded people of the man who had found adventure and happiness in the sky.